RAPTURE FLOATING ON PHANTOM SEA

POETRY

ANGELO SPIZZARRI

© 2017 Angelo Spizzarri
ALL RIGHTS RESERVED

www.SPIZZARRI.com

No part of this book may be reproduced or utilized in any form or by any means, electronic or mechanical, including photocopying, recording or by any information storage and retrieval system, without the prior written permission of the author.

Book page layout & cover by Spizzarri Entertainment Ltd.

PRINTED IN THE UNITED STATES OF AMERICA
THIS BOOK IS PRINTED ON ACID FREE PAPER

ISBN: 0-9779731-2-5

All words & Face logo: Angelo Spizzarri
Cover Art: Angelo Spizzarri
Photo: Jason Clay Oneal

WHEN YOU STOP
FIGHTING THE
STRAITJACKET
ITS GRIP LOOSENS

CONTENTS

1 EYES OF TWO
2 HALF FLOATING
3 BLEEDING WOUND
4 FLYING SOULS SLEEP
5 STAINED SKIN
6 CLOUDS KISS
7 CHILD OF THE SKY
8 SLEEP RAN AWAY FROM ME
9 THE NEW FLESH
10 A HEART
11 THE LAST TIME
12 MEMORY
13 SEARCHING
14 BROKEN
15 COLD
16 DISCONNECTED
17 RIP APART
18 SILENCE
19 WASTED
20 RAZORS ANGEL
21 THE STAR
22 THE TOWER
23 SLICED MOTH
24 BIRD
25 COLD WAVES
26 SLEEPWALKING
27 WANDERING
28 TIME
29 SURROUNDED
30 LA LUNA
31 MAZE
32 FLESH AND VEINS
33 SILENTLY STARVING
34 THE ARC OF TIME
35 GOLD
36 SNAKE
37 ANXIETY
38 SAC OF TEARS
39 WAVES
40 PHOENIX
41 DYSTOPIA
42 IMPALER
43 REBIRTH
44 HANGED MAN
45 ANGEL
46 ATMAN
47 ETERNAL
48 DESERT
49 FEEL
50 DESIRE
51 LET GO
52 LONELINESS
53 LAST HUMAN
54 DUSK
55 GLOW
56 ONCE, A TIME...
57 A RED STAR
58 A MOON
59 VOID
60 FEAR
61 IN THE WOMB
62 SERENITY AS FAR...
63 THE MOON AT NIGHT...
64 DISSOLVE
65 THE GREEN STARS
66 WISH
67 THE VICIOUS CIRCLE

CONTENTS CONTINUED

68 A CUT
69 THE TUNNEL
70 SECRETS
71 REVERBERATION OF GEIST
72 THE ORANGE MOON
73 CAMELS MARCHED
74 ASIAN DREAM
75 SNOW IS FALLING
76 SWIMMING IN THE WOMB
77 THE PAIN WE INFLICT
78 SQUEEZE THE NAKED FEVER
79 I USED TO SLEEP
80 THIS CLOUD
81 I REMEMBER
82 MY HEART
83 STARS ARE ECHOING
84 GHOST OF A HEART
85 THE CATERPILLAR
86 A QUARANTINED HEART
87 TWILIGHT OZONE
88 THE SHAKING
89 IN THE UNKNOWN
90 OPAL BEAMS
91 MEMORIES
92 FORGETTING DESIRE
93 I SHALL NEVER KNOW
94 I TRIED TO IMPLANT
95 OH PHANTOM
96 FROM MY BREATH BIRD SOAR
97 THE PHANTOM IS GONE
98 SO TORMENTING
99 THIS VESSEL
100 I RECALL

RAPTURE FLOATING ON PHANTOM SEA

POETRY

ANGELO SPIZZARRI

EYES OF TWO

EYES SHUT SEE
THE EYES OF TWO
SENSES SEVERED
SCREAMING TATTOO
RUNS THE HAND
ALONG THE THIGH
ON ALLEYS HIDDEN
IN SHANGHAI
WINDS SWIRL DOWN
FROM THE STARS
WITH YOUR TONGUE
YOU LICKED THE SCAR
SILENCE FLOATS IN
A WAVES EYE
BLIND AS LOVE
BREATHES AND SIGHS
SINKING SLEEP
FADES INTO
A HYBRID OF SOULS
THE EYES OF TWO

HALF FLOATING

HALF FLOATING
    ON FRACTURED
    SEA WAVES
SHE IS NUMB
    SHE IS NUMB
JAGGED FREEZE FRAME
RIPPLES IN TIME
    SHE IS HER HEART
IT IS FRACTURED UPON
THE STAR SHEEN
    SHE IS FROZEN
    SHE IS FROZEN
TOO MANY DREAMS
    THAT CAN BE HERS
BUT SHE DOESN'T
WANT THEM
    SHE IS NUMB
HALF FLOATING
    ON THE FRACTURED
    SEA WAVES

BLEEDING WOUND

IN MY HANDS THE BEATING PAIN
WRAPPED IN VEINS OF VAIN
CUT THE ARTERY
    KISSING
    PUMPING
THE PHANTOM INSANE

ALONE IN ISOLATION
FEELING SAFE
WEEPING IN THE SILENCE
    MY PAIN DOES NOT
    GO OUT IN TEARS

I SIT IN THE DARK HOLDING
THIS BEATING PAIN
    YOU SEE ITS MINE
    AND IT'S ALL I HAVE
THE BEATING LULLS ME TO SLEEP

BUT IT'S THE ONLY SOUND
THAT HALTS MY DREAMS

FLYING SOULS SLEEP

SWIMMING IN GREEN CLOUDS
ANGELS SOAR WITH WINGS
STARS SHIMMER AND CRY
HEARTS UPON THE FLOATING
OCEANS OF YESTERDAY
AURORA LIGHTS PIROUETTE
AND DANCE THROUGH THE EYE
OF FLIGHT WITH SOLAR
BIRDS OF PARADISE IN RIBBONS OF
FLUORESCENT SOUL SINGING SUNSET
WONDERS WHERE ARE THE EYES
THAT USED TO WATCH IT TO SLEEP
WHERE NO SPACE
NO DARK MATTER STAYS
THE ANGELS SWIM INTO ETERNITY
WITH THE STARS
THAT SHIMMER AND CRY

STAINED SKIN

STAINED IS THE SKIN
FROM FRACTURED
BRUISED MEMORIES
THAT BURN THE HEART
AND HURT THE HEART
RED BEATING RED
PAIN SEEN AND SAID
NUMB ARE THE EYES
THAT SEEN TOO MUCH
OF THINGS INSANE THAT
CAUSE THE PAIN
I DREAM AND SEE
WHAT I ONCE WAS
THE PAST IS GONE
BUT MY HEART
IS STILL STAINED
BUT ONLY I CAN SEE
WHERE IT'S STAINED

CLOUDS KISS

FROM EACH SIDES HORIZON
THE FLOATING CLOUDS
SOFTLY MOVE ACROSS
THE SILENT SKY
EYES CLOSED
LIPS NOT MOVING
THEY GLIDE TOWARDS
ONE ANOTHER
NO BARRIER COMPLEXED
AND HESITATIONS
AS DUSK COMES IN
THE ROSE AND AMBER
LIPS SOAR TO BLISS
AND INDIGO FALLS
FROM HIGH ABOVE
THE COULDS ABOUT
TO TOUCH BARELY MISS
AND CONTINUE ON NEVER
TO EMBRACE OR KISS
THE FIGURE STANDING
FAR DOWN BELOW
WATCHES IN QUIETUDE
WITH MOUNTAINS BEHIND
WALKS ON ALONE

CHILD OF THE SKY

SHE RIDES THE ATMOSPHERE
SITS ON THE SCALES
OF DRAGON CLOUD
BREATHING STARS LIKE FIRE
THE GIRL CHILD
REACHING FOR STARS
SHIMMERING GLISTENING
WITHIN THE SETTING
ORANGE BLOOD ORB
INSIDE GREEN HUES
OF FOREVER SKY
SHE GAZES UP
HIGH AND SMILES
TO A THOUSAND
FLYING DRAGONFLIES
MOVING LIKE A FLOCK
OF BIRDS IN UNISON
INTO THE DARK
MATTER AND BEYOND
SLUMBER SLEEPS
THE SKY AND SIGHS
THE CHILD DRIFTS TO
SING INTO TOMORROW

SLEEP RAN AWAY FROM ME

MY EYES MOVE LEFT TO RIGHT
IN A DANCE OF REM SLEEP
DREAMING THE SEA THAT SWALLOWS
MY NERVE ENDINGS ALIVE
A HUNDRED FINGERS AND HANDS
TOUCHING SENDING TRANSMISSIONS
OF ELECTRIC SEXUAL CONVULSIONS
SWARMING INTO ME
ALL OVER ME THROUGH ME
I LEAVE MYSELF AND SOAR
BEYOND THE COSMOS
UNTIL I AM REBORN
IN A BIRTH OF WET FLESH AND THEN…
AWAKENED EYES BLURRED AND CRIES
SLEEP RAN AWAY FROM ME

THE NEW FLESH

I CUT I RIP I TEAR
AT THIS CHEST
TO PULL AND
DISCONNECT
THIS HEART
BEATING
MY HEART
NEEDING AND
FEASTING
THIS WANTING
ANOTHER
HUMAN TO HAVE
TO BE VULNERABLE
IS SICK TO ME
I TRY TO DISASSEMBLE
MYSELF TO NOT
FEEL THE PAIN
BUT THIS HEART
KEEPS EVADING
MY HANDS
SOMETIMES
I CAN GET IT
AND SOMETIMES
I DON'T
THIS IS THE
NEW FLESH

A HEART

A HEART
NEVER GETS
BROKEN
THE SAME WAY
TWICE

THE LAST TIME

THE LAST TIME I SAW
MY SOUL IT WAS HURT
AND BEATEN
IT NEEDED SOMETHING
OUTSIDE OF ITSELF
BUT EVERYTHING I TRIED
WAS MISUSED AND ABUSED
BROKEN AND USED
I NEED TO FIND
SOMETHING SPIRITUAL
AND NOT MATERIAL
I HAVE TO RECONNECT
TO FIND THIS SADNESS
AND REPLACE IT AGAIN
WITH SELF LOVE

MEMORY

IT PAINS ME SO
THIS MEMORY
FROM THE PAST
IT'S LIKE A GNAWING
AT MY BRAIN MATTER
ANXIETY CRUSHING AT TIMES
WHISPERING AT OTHERS

SPEAKING IN TONGUES
OF DISTANT LANDS
IT SEES ME IT WATCHES ME
AND WAITS AS I BREATHE

WHEN IT SLEEPS
IT STANDS AT THE EDGE
OF THE SEA AND CAUSES
RIPPLES IN THE WATER
OF SLEEP

SEARCHING

EVERY WAKING MOMENT
I AM SEARCHING FOR MYSELF
INSIDE THE DREAM TURNED
REVERSED AND UPSIDEDOWN

THE BABY IN MIND MOVES ITS MOUTH
BUT UTTERS NO SOUND MUTE
THERE IS SOMETHING IT HAS TO SAY
IT JUST DOESN'T KNOW HOW

I WILL SPEND MY WHOLE LIFE
FINDING THAT THING THE
INNER CHILD WANTS
SO DESPERATELY
TO SAY

BROKEN

BROKEN SHARDS
OF MIRRORS
RUBBING TOGETHER
INSIDE MY SOUL

THE FEELING
KEEPS ME
AWAKE AND
AWARE

IT'S THE LIVING
AND BREATHING
SCREAMING FROM
ALL OVER MY SKIN

ANXIETY I LOVE YOU

COLD

THIS HAND KNOWS
NO WARMTH OF LOVE
IT WENT AWAY YEARS AGO
THE FINGERTIPS BLUE
TRY TO HOLD ON TO
MY HEART SO MUCH
BUT THIS COLD BURNS
THIS SKIN NUMBS ME
THESE FINGERPRINTS
CRY ANOTHER TYPE OF TEAR
MY EYES THAT STARE DOWN
AT THIS HEART ARE HARD
AND SAD FILLED
I TRY NOT TO LOOK
BACK IN ANGER
SOMETIMES I JUST
CAN'T HELP IT

DISCONNECTED

ANGELS ARE FLOATING
AWAY FROM ME
I AM TOO INFECTED
THE BURNING OF
THIS TATTERED
AND TORN SELF
CANNOT REMAIN NON
NON – SANE INSANE
THE SENSES SEVERED
SLICED FLESH BUT
NO BLOOD POURS
FROM THE WOUND
OF DISCONNECTION
AND I DO NOT CRY
BECAUSE THIS SEEMS
TOO PERMANENT TO
LEAVE ME

RIP APART

TEAR ME RIP APART
THIS FLESH TEAR IT OUT
THESE ACHING NERVES
THAT HURT

DIG INTO MY HEART
SMASH IT OPEN TO
FIND MY SADNESS
MY PAIN

CUT OPEN THIS
DIMENSIONAL RIFT
AND LOCATE THIS SOUL
TO CLEANSE THESE STAINS
OF BLACK AND BLUE
BUT EVEN THEN
WILL I BE FREE?

SILENCE

WATCHING THE
LEAVES CHANGE
THEY FALL FROM
BRANCHES TO
THE GROUND
WHILE THEY FALL
THERE IS A SILENCE
THAT IS THE
SOUND OF TIME

WASTED

TIME NEVER
TELLS YOU
ABOUT ALL
THE MOMENTS
YOU'VE WASTED
UNTIL IT'S
TOO LATE

RAZORS ANGEL

THE RAZORS SURROUND US
ANGELS ON THE LEFT FIGHTING
WITH ANGELS ON THE RIGHT
JABBING FISTS AND ANGRY
WIND FROM WINGS
FLESH BRUISED AND
HEARTS HURT OF WHO ONCE
WERE CLOSE NOW
FOREVER ENEMIES
VULTURES SOAR OVER
THE WAR TORN PLAINS
OF ONE AGAINST ONE
UNTIL IT ENDS
THE RAZORS STILL
SURROUND US

THE STAR

SWIMMING IN THE
INDIGO BLUE THE STAR
PIROUETTES AND GLIDES
IN APERTURE IT TUMBLES
THROUGH THE DARK MATTER
THAT SUSPENDS IT
POURING ITS ESSENCE
IT SPILLS ITS LIGHT FROM
ITS MAGMA WHICH WILL TRAVEL
EONS TO REACH ANY BEING
TO RECEIVE IT
TIME CANNOT
COUNT THE EONS
IT WILL TAKE
WHEN IT DOES REACH
A DESTINATION
IT WILL BE DEAD
BUT NO ONE WILL KNOW
FOR EONS TO COME

THE TOWER

HANGING FROM THE IONOSPHERE
THE TOWER STANDS MOTIONLESS
FROM THE GASEOUS CLOUDS
IT IS BUILT FROM MY LIES
UPSIDEDOWN MY TOWER OF BABEL
ONE WHO STEPS OFF ITS EDGE
ITS SURFACE WILL FALL REVERSED
INTO THE CENTER PULLED
UP AND TO THE UNIVERSE
WHEN YOU GAZE INTO
THE HORIZON IT SPEAKS
BACKWARDS TO YOUR MIND
OF YOUR MEMORIES OF THE PAST
YOU HAD FORGOTTEN AND
WISHED YOU NEVER REMEMBERED
AGAIN THEIR SHADOWS

SLICED MOTH

SLICING ITS OWN WINGS
WITH ANY RAZOR
IT SAW FIT TO USE
IT BELIEVED WITH
THE PRAYERS OF THE MANY
FROM THE CITY IN THE DISTANCE
EMERGING FROM THE SHATTERED
CRACK WITHIN THE MATTER
SLIGHTLY HANGING IN THE SKY
THAT IT CAN AND WILL
REACH THE CITY
THE MOTH DID AS IT HEARD
HE TRIED TO USE THESE WORDS
TO FLY UP AND INTO THE
SHIMMERING GOLDEN CITY
JUST OUT OF REACH
BUT NO MATTER HOW HARD
IT PRAYED IT COULDN'T
GET INTO THE CITY
IT HAD THE MEANS
BUT LISTENED TO THE
FAKE OUTER FORCE
INSTEAD OF THE TRUE INNER

BIRD

A BIRD FLEW DOWN
AND BEGAN TO ATTACK
A PAIR OF LUNGS
HANGING FROM
A TREE OF LONELINESS
IN A DESERT

THE LUNGS SPOKE
WITH WINDS THAT SAID
IF YOU DEVOUR ANY
PART OF ME I SHALL DIE

THE BIRD SAID NOTHING AND
CONTINUED TO PICK AND TEAR
AND CLAW THE PINK FLESH

AFTER THE LUNGS WERE DEAD
THE BIRD FLEW AWAY WITHOUT
ANY THOUGHT OF THE
LUNGS IT JUST FED UPON

I GUESS THE BIRD SPOKE
ANOTHER LANGUAGE

COLD WAVES

COLD WAVES
CRASHING
AGAINST THE
CONCRETE EDGE
MY HANDS ARE
COLD IN THE WIND
THE PURPLE BLACK SKY
STINGS MY EYES MAKING
TEARS CRY OUT IN PAIN

UNENDING ARE THE WAVES
ANXIETY CLUTCHES MY CHEST
AMBER LIGHTS REFLECT
BACK TO CLOUDS
I STAND AND FEEL MY
TEARS CRY OUT IN PAIN
BUT THIS DAMAGED
HEART ISN'T HERE
IT'S SOMEWHERE ELSE
RELIVING THE PAST

SLEEPWALKING

THE WAVES ARE SLEEPING
NO RIPPLES NO MOVEMENT
IN THE WATER OF THIS SEA
HUSH NOW YOU'LL WAKE
THEN THE SILENCE

NO SLEEPWALKING
IN MY DREAMS
CAUSE I DREAMWALK
EVERY DAY

AT NIGHT OPAL BEAMS
REFLECT BACK EMOTIONS
THAT CANNOT BE
THEY'RE NOT
NEEDED ANYMORE
FOR THE PAIN
IS SLEEPING
WITH THE WAVES
AND THE SILENCE

WANDERING

WHERE IS THIS
GROAN GOING
IT IS LOST IN
BACKWARDS STATE
LEFT CAST ASIDE
FROM A FEELING
IT CAN'T REMEMBER
ANYMORE
WITH THIS GROAN
IS A SILENCE
SLEEPING

THAT'S WHERE
ITS DREAMS OF
LOVE ARE KEPT
HIDDEN

TIME

A TREE SITS
INBETWEEN
A TIME
I STAND THERE
HEARING ITS
WHISPERS
WIND MOVING
ITS FINGERTIPS
THERE ARE
NO LEAVES

INBETWEEN
HAS TURNED TO
TOMORROW
THE TREE STILL
STANDS AND SPEAKS
IN WHISPERS

I LISTEN
BUT I DO NOT
UNDERSTAND

SURROUNDED

RAZORS SURROUND
A BLUE ANGEL
IN STILL SPACE
THE BLADES ARE
BURNING FLASHING AS
A BODY LIES IN WAITING
IT IS SICK BUT IT DOES
NOT WANT ANY MEDICATION
THE HEAT IS THERE
TO REMIND THEM OF
THE LIMITATIONS OF
EXISTENCE
THE METAL DOESN'T
KNOW A SECRET
ONE LYING IN WAITING
ONLY KNOWS
NON – LIMITS
OF ITS MIND
BUT WAITS FOR
A PILL A CURE
THAT DOES
NOT EXIST

LA LUNA

LA LUNA SHE
ILLUMINATES MY
VEINS AND MY MIND
HER LIGHT IT
MAKES VISIBLE
ANOTHER KIND OF SIGHT
LA LUNA
SHE SINGS A
SONG ONLY I CAN HEAR
HER LIGHT CAN
ERASE ALL THE
TENSION AND FEAR
LA LUNA SHE
KNOWS ONLY
THE RIGHT WAY
SHE SINGS A
SONG TO HELP ME
WHEN I HAVE
NOTHING TO SAY

MAZE

WHERE IS YOUR FACE
I DON'T KNOW
ILL HAVE TO FIND IT
BUT THE MIRROR
HAS SECRETS
AND THE BRAIN A MAZE
I TRY AND TRY BUT MY
HANDS KEEP SLIDING
DOWN THE SAME HALLS
SOMEWHERE TO LONELINESS
CONFUSION DROOLS FROM
MY MOUTH IN SALIVA
VOICES PLAY WITH MY MIND
CAUSE I ALLOW THEM TO
UNTIL I FORGET WHAT I WAS
SEARCHING FOR
AND THE SEARCHING
BECOMES THE ONLY
THING I KNOW

FLESH AND VEINS

FLESH ANGELS BLEED
WITH BLEEDING HEARTS
BEATING WITH VEINS
OF EMOTIONS DEFECTED
FROM GHOSTS IN THE PAST
THEY FLOAT ON NOT FEELING
THE PAST BUT THESE ANGELS
PUMPING WITH THIS
LIFE BLOOD AND FLESH FEEL
IT CAUSES SEIZURES
THESE MEMORIES
THE ANGELS DON'T KNOW
WHAT THEY ARE BUT
SLEEP DOESN'T COME IN
THEIR LIMBO THIS AFTERMATH
STILL THEY BLEED DEEPLY

SILENTLY STARVING

CRYING THE TREE OF ARTERY
IS STARVING FOR A FOOD
A SUSTENANCE OF SOME KIND
DANCING IN THE MIST
THE BUTTERFLIES ATTRACTED
BY ITS LIGHT ALMOST
FLUORESCENT HAZE INDIGO
THEY LAND UPON THE
BARREN FINGER LIKE BRANCHES
ONE BY ONE THE ARTERY
SUCKS AND LEECHES
THEIR SMALL LIVES AWAY
SLOWLY IN JAGGED TIME LAPSE
DRY FLOATING WINGS FALL
AS SILENT AS YAWNS THROUGH
THE FAINT SLOW MOTION BREEZE
ONE BY ONE FALL THEY LAND
THE GLOW NOW SEES

THE ARC OF TIME

TRAVELING THROUGH A DISTANT TIME
AN ARC SET SAIL ACROSS SEVEN SEAS
TO FIND THE FABRIC OF TIME
A FOURTH DIMENSION TO OTHERS
WHERE THEY COULD LIVE FOREVER
THE ANGEL, MOTH AND A SLEEPING CHILD
WERE ALL THERE TO SEEK AND POSSESS
THIS GOD LIKE PIECE OF MATERIAL PLANE
MANY EONS PASSED IN SEARCH
THE ARC PASSED THE MANY PLACES
ZONE OF SPHERES AND STARS
BUT THEY CRIED FOR THIS SOJOURN
SEEMED TO IMMENSE TO COMPLETE
GASES OF CLOUDS AND
SEAS OF MATTER PASSED
INTO THIS FOREVER SEAM
OF THE CONSTRUCT OF TIME
THE ARC CONTINUED ENDLESSLY
THE FABRIC OF TIME CAN BE STRETCHED
BUT CANNOT BREAK OR BE FOUND

GOLD

IN THE LOST DUNES
OF SUN BLEACHED WHITE
STOOD A SOLID TOWER OF GOLD
THAT DAZZLED THE
CURIOUS ONES EYES
AS THE SUN SIZZLED HIS MIND
HE FOUND HIMSELF BEFORE THIS
MASSIVE MONOLITH AND SOMETHING
THAT RESEMBLED A DOOR
THAT WAS SEALED SHUT
HE FELT DEEP INSIDE SO SURE
THE DOOR WOULD OPEN
AND GIVE HIM THE PRECIOUS WATER
HE DESPERATELY THIRSTED FOR THAT
HE PRAYED AND PRAYED WITH WANT
A DEEP WANT THAT MADE DESIRE STRONG
TIME PASSED AND THE SUN BEAMED DOWN
WHERE HE DIED IN THE SINKING
SHADOW OF THE TOWER OF GOLD

SNAKE

A MAN SLEPT
ONE NIGHT AND HAD
AN UNSPEAKABLE DREAM
HIS HUMAN BODY HAD
TRANSFORMED INTO
THAT OF A SNAKE
HE MOVED SLITHERED
WITH SKIN AND SCALE
AND FORKED TONGUE
BLOOD COLD AND NUMB
SHEDDING SELF FOR OTHERS
FEAR STRUCK AND HE AWOKE
RELIEF WASHING OVER
AS ANXIETY MORPHED
TO DREAM SLEEP
THE SNAKE BECAME
AWAKE AND AWARE
THAT HE NOW LIVED
LAYING UPON THE
HOT ROCK IT SLEPT

ANXIETY

BLACK ANTS MARCH
AROUND IN MY
MIND LIKE ANXIETY
WORKING OVERTIME
CIRCLING SURROUNDING
THE PUPPET MASTERED
BY THE STRINGS OF
EVERYTHING UNTIL
I AM CONSUMED
THIS TIGHTNESS
IN MY CHEST WHERE
THIS HEART RESTS
INSIDE A PRISON
OF SELF BY THE SELF
I AM JUDGE JURY
AND EXECUTIONER
EXECUTING MY DEMISE
ALMOST PERFECTLY

SAC OF TEARS

BLUE DOG OF FU
SITTING WITHIN THIS
GARDEN OF EDEN
KEEPING GUARD OVER
THE TISSUE MEMBRANE
A SAC OF SALTY TEARS
FROM THE PAST FAILURES
AND WRONG PERCEPTIONS
MASKS FALSE AND LIES SAID
WHAT I WAS TOLD TO BE
AND WHAT I NEVER WAS
THE FLOWERS ARE
FLOATING AND FRAGRANT
THE SOFT MUTED HUE
OF SKIES ETERNAL
THE DOG OF FU STARES
AND IS ALARMED GROWLING
IT CAN'T BE ABOUT ME?

WAVES

AURA BLISTER OF
PRIMARY COLOR
STREAK ACROSS THE
FACE OF MOON
PULLING TO MOVING
THE OCEAN WAVES
BELOW THE PULSING
GLOWING LIVING CITY
WAVE AFTER CRASHING WAVE
THEY SPEAK TO EACH OTHER
A FOREIGN LANGUAGE
I WAS NEVER TO
EVER UNDERSTAND
I WISH TO COMMUNICATE
WITH THE OCEAN
A SHAKING HAND
I TASTE THE LIQUID
HOW STRANGE IT TASTES
LIKE SALTY BITTER TEARS
YES – HOW STRANGE

PHOENIX

THE CRIMISON PHOENIX
FLEW DOWN FROM DAWNS
MOUNTAIN IN ATMOSPHERE
WHERE IT WITNESSED
THE BONES OF SOMETHING
A GHOST IT ONCE HEARD OF
THIS BEING LIKE PARASITE
USED WHAT IT NEEDED
THEN WOULD DISPOSE
IT WHEN FINISHED
AND THEN REPEAT
GLANCING WITH SLIGHT FEAR
AT THE SCENE FROM THE
SHORES OF GREEN BAMBOO
IT CRIED ONLY ONE TEAR
THAT WAS ALL AND THEN
TURNED CALLED TO ITS ECHO
AND FLEW BACK UP AND AWAY
TOWARDS SAFETY OF SUN
THE BONES AFTER ALL
IN THE END WERE HUMAN

DYSTOPIA

THE SKELETAL HORSE
MARCHED THROUGH
ITS OWN DYSTOPIA
THE GROUND EATEN
BLASTED BY EXPLOSION
MOUNTAIN AND TREE
CONSUMED BY IMPLOSION
FAR IN THE HAZE GRAY
COVERED DISTANCE
A CITY DESERTED STOOD
OPEN MAW OF CAVITY AS IF
TIME FORGOT WHAT IT FORGOT
STANDING UPON A CLIFF
OF RIPPED EARTH IT SAW
BONES OF THE MANY
SMASHED AND PULVERIZED
FROM FORCES DESTRUCTIVE
NOTHING COULD
HAVE STOPPED IT
HATE HAD FINALLY WON
HEAD DOWN THE
WAR TORN HORSE
MARCHED ON INTO
A FOURTH DIMENSION

IMPALER

A BED OF NAILS
RAZOR THIN NEEDLES
READY TO SINK INTO
THIS PALE FLESH
THAT LAYS DOWN
TO SLEEP TO SLUMBER
IMPALER FILL MY BODY
WITH INJECTION STEEL
TO FUSE ME TO THIS ZONE
THIS COMFORT ZONE
THIS BLEAK EMPTY ZONE
A BLIND NUMB ZONE
I AM IN FEAR TO LEAVE
PLEASE I WANT TO STAY
MY FLESH WOUNDED
GROWS NEW SKIN OVER
THE NEEDLE STEEL UNTIL
I CAN NO LONGER SEE
WHERE THEY ARE
ANYMORE

REBIRTH

ALL KNOWING EYE APPEARS
SUSPENDED HIGH IN THE SKY
BELOW ON GRAY SLATE PLAINS
A RIVER STYX LEADS ANY SEEKING
THE ALL SEEING EYE OF KNOWING
RED BIRD DELICATE FAST FLEW UP
TO ASK FOR DIRECTION IN ITS LIFE
FEAR LACED MIND IN CONFUSION
DOUBT FILLING A BEATING HEART
THE ALL KNOWING EYE GAVE
IT WHAT THIS TINY BIRD NEEDED
IN AN INSTANT IT SEIZED DROPPED
FALLING TO THE GROUND IN DEATH
SILENCE ENTERED THE SPAN THEN
LIKE NOTHING THE EYE WAS GONE
SOMETIMES ONE DOESN'T KNOW
TRULY WHAT ONE IS ASKING FOR

HANGED MAN

A STONE TREE SITS IN
A FOURTH DIMENSION
REMAINS OF MANGLED FORM
DISTORTED FROM LIGHTNING
BLAST FROM AN ANGER STORM
PALE MAN WAS THERE HANGING
DOWNSIDE UP FROM THE
ARM OF A PETRIFICATION
BOUND BLIND WITH DELUSION
UNSURE HE WONDERED WHY
HE WAS THERE AND WHEN
THIS ODD STATE WOULD END
DEFECTS OF CHARACTER
NEGATED PUMPED IN VEINS
SALIVATING DRAINED FROM LIPS
THE RAZOR INSIDE HIS CHEST
WOULD RELEASE HIM BUT
HE HAD NOT STRENGTH TO
FIGHT DEFECTS TO HELP HIMSELF
AS THE EON TICKED THROUGH
DUST BEGAN TO GATHER UPON HIM
IT WAS THEN HE STARTED TO FEAR

ANGEL

FLAMES WHIRLED WRITHED
COMBUSTION RACING OOZING
DOWN FROM VOLCANO SPARKING
RIVERS LIQUID MAGMA CHARRING
SPACE FACELESS ANGEL OCCUPIED
STOOD TRYING TO FREE HIS WINGS
WHICH WERE BOUND BY STEEL LEAD
IF THE LEAD WERE MELTED FREEING
HIS WINGS THE FEATHER AND FLESH
WOULD SURELY TURN TO ASH CINDER
FACELESS ONE WANTED DEPERATELY
TO BE FREE BUT IT WOULD MEAN
ROAMING TO WANDER THIS HELL HEAT
THIS FIRE CHOKED BLACK VISTA
WITH ALL ABANDONED THOUGHT
FACELESS ONE FELL BACK UPON
THE WHITE MOLTEN SINUOUS LAVA
BURNING AWAY HIS WINGS HIS FREEDOM
GOING FROM ONE SELF MADE PRISON
TO ANOTHER SOMETIMES HAS TO BE

ATMAN

MORPHING CLOUDS IN FLUCTUATION
SWIRLING IN FAST FRAME ANIMATE
ATMAN ESSENCE EXISTED IN HIS SELF
IMPERISHABLE STATE NO SENSES
CAN REACH HIM BUT A NON – DUAL
STATE OF SELF – ABSORPTION
SEA OF SKIES SHAPED HUES TINTED
LIVING BREATHING SUN RISE AND SET
INDIVIDUAL BEYOND PHENOMENA
CHRONOS CAN NOT BE HERE FOR THIS
A DIMENSION OF INNER PURE SELF IS
MOST RADIANT UNAFFECTED BY EGO
SYNTHESIZED OF HIGH CONSCIOUSNESS
A REALITY WITHOUT MATTER OR ANTI
ONE WILL SPEND ONES LIFE FORCE
TO ACHIEVE THIS ETERNAL EVER STATE
FREE FROM NEGATION OF PERCEPTION
ABSENCE OF DESIRE A MIND KILLER

ETERNAL

COSMOS SILENT AS STAR SCREAM
RIPPLES IN THE OCEAN OF SENSES
THE COSMIC EGG FLOATS IN LIMBO
DARK MATTER SURROUNDS THE SPAN
VISHNU SITS IN QUIETUDE AND SELF
INSIDE THE ORB OF THIN SHELL THE
LIQUID OF THE ETERNAL AWAITS
FOR THE RIGHT CHRONOS TO BIRTH
THE OM – AT THE CENTER VOID
SURGES A MOST POWERFUL FORCE
VISHNU OBSERVES THE EGG DEEPLY
INTENSELY NOTICING A CRACK IN
ITS SURFACE WHERE LIQUID HAS
LEAKED FROM TREMOR OF VOID
VISHNU OBSERVED THE FRAIL SHELL
SHATTER WHERE THE OM IS NOW BORN
RELEASED FROM THE TRUE INFINITE
ONE HAS NO CONTROL OVER CHANGE
EVEN IF ONE IS READY FOR IT OR NOT

DESERT

DUSK FELL UPON SAND DUNES
A DESERT DESERTED BY CHRONOS
THE ECLIPSED MOON HANGS OVER
CLOSE TO HORIZONS LINE WITHIN
A NET OF GLIMMERING STARS AFAR
A CRAB CRAWLED UNAWARE OF A
CHRONOS MISSING HERE IN SPACE
EACH STEP AND SMALL HILL OF SAND
WAS A STRUGGLE SCALING MOUNTAINS
SOMETIMES HE WOULD FALL ROLLING
OVER AND FOUGHT TO RIGHT HIMSELF
TO CONTINUE THIS SOJOURN TO A
PLACE THE CRAB WOULD NEVER KNOW
OR FIND BUT STILL HE CRAWLED ON
NEVER KNOWING THAT TIME DID NOT
EXIST AND LIFE FORCE IS UNENDING
BUT PURPOSE WAS NOT FOR THIS
CREATURE FOR IT WOULD NEVER
KNOW WHAT PURPOSE REALLY WAS

FEEL

THE LUSH LOTUS HOVERS OVER
SEA OF TRANQUILITY ITS SCENT
BLOOMS WITH SERENITY PEACE
FROM THE CENTER A THOUSAND
ARMS AND A THOUSAND HANDS
TO SEARCH OUT A MEANING TO
FEEL EVERY POSSIBLE DIMENSION
OF REALITY DEEP VIBRATING CORE
IT WANTED FOR MORE BUT IT KNEW
TO FEEL SEARCH OUT TO SEEK OUT
BUT NEVER TO KNOW WHY AND TO
WHAT END AS LAPPING RIPPLES OF
WAVES CRASHED IN SLOW MOTION
THE HANDS HAD LIMITATIONS BUT
LIMITATIONS WERE A STATE THAT
ONE WHO SEARCHES BLINDLY AND
ENDLESSLY WILL NEVER KNOW

DESIRE

THE SKY WAS LOW WITH GREEN MIST
THE PLACE WAS FILLED OF MOUNTAIN
MESA SHADOWS CRAWLED THROUGH
DISPLAYED FROM STEEL BEAMS WERE
MANY SKINS USED FLESH OF HUMAN
ALL HAD CROWNS THORNS FASTENED
TO MANY HEADS CRIMSON BLOOD THIN
TRAILS STAINED WHITE SKIN LIKE RAZOR
CUTS FROM FUSED PAIN AND PLEASURE
BREEZES BLEW IN FROM NOWHERE
THE SKINS MOVED SLIGHTLY IN WIND
MAKING ALL WRITHE IN DEMENTED
DANCING OF WICKED FEVER FRENZY
THIS WAS AN UNREST PLACE FOR THEM
SORROW EXISTS HERE UNAFFECTED
FOR THEIR CORRUTPED HEART MINDS
DISASSOCIATION FROM REAL LIFE
THEY HANG HERE FOR THE TASTE WAS
TOO IMMENSE THIS DESIRE OVER RIDING
SENSES UNTIL PARALYSIS POISONED
CAUSE IT COULD NOT FILL THEIR THRIST
NO MORE SO IN PRISON NOW THEY WAIT

LET GO

SOMEWHERE IN SPACE OF SPHERES
ANYWHERE NOWHERE IN DARKNESS
HUMAN STOOD NAKED FLESH WRAPPED
IN BARBWIRE FIXING HIM TO THE SPOT
ATOP A HILL YELLOW SUNLIGHT DRONE
THESE RAZORS DIGGING IN HIM HURT
CAUSING HIM EMOTIONAL PAIN AS WELL
HE WOULD NOT LET GO OF THE PAST
HOW DESPERATELY HE WANTED TO BE
FREE OF THIS PHYSICAL EMOTIONAL
NEGATED STATE HE COULD NOT FREE
HIS INNER MIND TO RELEASE HIS BONDS
HE COULD EXIST FREE FROM DEFECTS
HIS MEMORY RECALLED A TIME HE DID
TEARS CAME FROM THE PAST FREEDOM
THAT ONCE WAS AND COULD BE AGAIN
IF PRESENT COULD RELEASE PAST TO
RIGHT HIS FUTURE IF ONLY HE LET GO

LONELINESS

WITHIN TREES OF HUSHED SECLUSION
BRIGHT GREEN FOLIAGE BREATHING
SAT LARGE WHITE SILK FETAL COCOON
UNBORN CATHARSIS HIDING OUT
FROM PAIN PLEASURE EVERYTHING
INSIDE FETAL HUMAN HELD TREMBLING
IN HANDS A RAZOR TO CUT THE COCOON
OPEN SO HE CAN BE FREE TO LIVE BUT
FEAR QUICKENED HIS HEART BEAT
RACED PUMPING BLOOD INSIDE PINK
WALLS OF SAFE GAUZY TRANSLUCENSE
RAPID CHANGE PUPA TO IMAGO CAN'T
METAMORPHOSE FOR FETAL HUMAN
CANNOT USE THE RAZOR TO FREE
HIMSELF FROM THIS BIRTHING FOR
THE UNKOWN WAS MORE FEARED
THEN THE KNOWN AND HE WAS SAFE
INSIDE THIS COCOON BUT IF FETUS
DID NOT FREE HIMSELF HE WOULD
DIE WITHIN THESE WALLS AND NEVER
KNOW A BEAUTIFUL LIFE EXPERIENCE

LAST HUMAN

A METAL FRAME CUBE EXISTS
BROKEN BLACK MOUNTAINS LACE
THIS WASTELAND AND HERE THE
FLUORESCENT MOON A LIGHT SOURCE
HOLDING A LONE PRISONER OF SELF
LAST HUMAN KNEELING ON GLASS
METAL SPIKES CONNECTED TO
THE TOP CUBE FRAME IN UNISON
ENTER THE HUMAN BRAIN MATTER
FIXING THE HEAD TO THE SPACE
IT CANNOT MOVE IT CANNOT EXIT
BUT IT CAN FEEL AND IT IS IN PAIN
PUNISHMENT OF THIS SELF PRISON
HE NEVER FELT WORTH ANYONE OR
ANYTHING SINCE IN UTERO POISON
FILLING HIS MIND OF ALTERED SELF
PERCEPTION WHERE HE GAVE INTO
HIS FALSE MIND EYE THIS CORRUPTED
SELF EYE BUT INDEED HE HAD A WAY
OUT BUT HE DIDN'T UNDERSTAND HOW
ACCEPTANCE WAS A WAY TO FREE SELF

DUSK

ON THE SEA OF YESTERDAY WAVES
WHISPER TO ONE ANOTHER AS THEY
OBSERVE THE ARC IN ITS FINAL TRIP
A RAFT FLOATS NOT FAR BARING A
LONE DEAD TREE OF THORNS THE PYRE
IS SET THE FUNERAL READY TO BEGIN
EVERYONE WAS THERE IN NEGATION
BAD DREAM RAGE AND FEAR WERE NEAR
DEPRESSION ANXIETY ARM AND ARM
WORTHLESSNESS HAD ITS ARM AROUND
EGO WHO HAD TEARS IN ITS HURT EYES
DESIRE ALSO BLEAK MOTION LIFELESS
ALL BUT LONELINESS WAS NOT THERE
ALL STOOD REMEMBERING AS THE ONE
RED AND ONE BLUE BUTTERFLY ABOVE
COMMENCED AND AS ALL GAZED OUT
TO THE SEA THE RAFT STARTS TO BURN
FIRST SLOW THEN WILDFIRE LICKING
THE BUTTERFLIES CRIED SILENTLY AS
THEY FLEW AND WATCHED THE SCENE
THEN NO ONE WAS LEFT ONE BY ONE
THEY ALL PAID THEIR RESPECTS FOR
THIS TIME THIS LAST TIME NOW DONE
QUIETLY THE TINY RED AND BLUE ONES
LANDED SOFTLY STARED DEAD AHEAD
THE ARC SAILED INTO THE DEEP DUSK

GLOW

FLUORESCENT BLUB
FLICKERING SICK SUN
SO ILL AND FINAL
YOUR LIGHT
GOES NO WHERE
LIMITATIONS BURDENS
TOO PRIMAL
SHINE ON HEALTHY
SKIN A WHITE SLUG
BELLY GLOW
THAT CAN'T GROW
LIFE UNLAST NOT
SAD TO SHOW
IT'S THE ONLY
WAY YOU KNOW

ONCE, A TIME…

ONE DAY SOME ROBOTIC INSECTS
FOUND THE SKIN OF TIME
NOT KNOWING WHAT TO DO WITH IT
HUNG IT ON A WALL TO DRY
AS THEY SAW IT WOULD NOT DRY
THEY BLOTTED AWAY THE LIQUID
NOT KNOWING THAT IT WAS WET
FROM NOT WATER BUT TEARS
THEY WENT ABOUT THEIR WAYS
ON THE WALL THERE IT STAYED
ONLY TENDED TO WHEN EVER
IT WAS NEEDED AS PERIODIC
AS MOMENT TO PASSED BY MOMENT
ALTHOUGH MOIST IT STAYED

A RED STAR

FLOATING FAR IN
OILY EBONY NIGHT
A MILLION TRILLION
MILES AWAY FLIGHT
PULSATING AS IF A HEART
RED STAR SHINES
MYSTERIOUS ALARMED
NO ONE KNOWS THE
LOVE LIGHTS LENGTH TRAVEL
LIFE FORCE SOOTHING
THE ELEMENTAL
STILL A VACUUM A STILLNESS
BLACK WINDS
SILENT AND WRITHE
THRASHING WINDS
A RED STAR BREATHES
RELENTLESS AND GLOWS
BY AND BY

A MOON

FLUORESCENT SKIN
IN THE SKY
GLAZING SO PLACID
WAY UP HIGH
IN THE BURNING
COLD PALE NIGHT
FROM WHERE DOES
YOUR DESIRE RISE?

VOID

FLYING HIGH THROUGH
EMPTINESS AND SHADOWS
WILL I FIND MY WAY TO
THE ONLY PORTAL HOME
SCREAMS RUN AROUND
INSIDE MY VEINS
TAP THE VEINS AND SEE
MY SOUL FLOW AWAY
IN BEAMS OF RADIANT PURE
ANGELIC WHITE LIGHT
I'M EMPTY AND WITHERING
AWAY SLOWLY DRIPPING
MELTING NEVER
FINDING ANYTHING
ALONE

FEAR

FEAR CANNOT
WALK ALONE
IT NEEDS A
COMPANION
WITHOUT ONE
IT DIES

IN THE WOMB

ALL IS TRANQUIL AND SURREAL
WARMTH OF THE SUN CARESSES
EVERY MILLIMETER OF FLESH
ALL IS PEACEFUL
THE OUTSIDE WORLD CANNOT
SEEP IN ITS CONFUSING PERPLEXITIES
I CAN KEEP MY SECRETS SAFE
HOT WHITE RAYS UPON MY FACE
CLEAR THOUGHTS
NO LURKING SHADOWS
CANNOT CONSUME
ALL IS CALM
ALL IS SUBDUED
I'M IN THE WOMB
IN THE WOMB

SERENITY AS FAR AS THE EYE CAN SEE

THE DANCE OF THE PALM TREES
BATHING IN LAVENDER
PEACH SUN GLOW
SHELTERED IN SAFETY
OF MOUNTAIN WALL
AND IT OPENED UP FOR US
THE SEA OF AMBER TRANQUILITY
WAVES OF SOLITUDE
LAPPING UPON THE ANGELS KISS
PALM TREES IN MOUNTAINS EMBRACE
EYES CLOSED FALLING FAST
TO SANE TO SLEEP
INK BLUE HUE WISPS
SLIDE INTO VIEW
DUSK LAYS A HAND
WITHOUT A SOUND
OVER THE DESERT LAND

THE MOON AT NIGHT BORN DEEP FROM THE WOMB OF THE MOUNTAINS

THESE EYES DRIP MY WASTED SOUL
FROM A THOUSAND YEARS AGO
MOON RISING ABOVE DARK HILLS
A DEEP INDIGO HORIZON
INK MIDNIGHT CLOUD CAME
FROM EITHER SIDE
ITS FINGERS REACHING ACROSS
CLASPING THE MOON IN AN EMBRACE
THEY GAVE FOND FARWELLS
AND SOON LET THE ORB
ASCEND HIGH INTO THE NIGHT
A GLISTENING BIRD
OF TWINKLING LIGHT
TOUCHED THE MOONS EDGE
WHILE AN AMBER SEA SHONE
FROM BELOW PULSED
VIBRATIONS MOVING BRIGHT
IT LET ME KNOW THAT I'M NOT
THE ONLY ONE HERE IN THIS WORLD

DISSOLVE

"WHERE ARE YOU?"
WE CAN'T HEAR YOU
CAUSE I'M IN THE ROOM
OF DISSOLVING WALLS
ALL IS STILL IN MY EYES
AS MY SIGHT DISSOLVES
WE FEEL THE HUM OF
ELECTRIC BLOOD COURSE
THROUGH MY VEINS
THE SPARK THAT IGNITES
THE FRICTION THAT
DISMEMBERS MY SOUL
TO REASSEMBLE AND
MAKE US WHOLE
FOR THERE IS NO
MORE SADNESS
AND SORROW
THERE IS ONLY ME NOW
ME AND MY SOUL
AND I'M CONTENT

THE GREEN STARS

THE APPARENT GREEN STARS
IN THE GREEN SKY HIGH ABOVE
MY EYES AND SOUL PULL GENTLY
AT MY HEART IN TUNE WITH MY SOUL
THE CRACKED MIRROR SHARDS
RUB AGAINST EACH SHARP EDGE
IN MY EYES DIZZYING ME IN RAPTURE
LOVE METAMORPHOSED
IN MY VEINS MAKES ME AWARE
OF THE FLUTTERING GREEN STARS
IN THE GREEN SKY HIGH ABOVE ME
AND THEIR PALE GREEN LIGHT
WHICH BEDAZZLES MY EYES

WISH

THE VEIL OF HAZE
WASHED OVER THE DAY
    BLACK
    SPASMING
THE BIRD SOARED AWAY
I ALWAYS WANTED
TO DO SOMETHING
WITH MY LIFE
AS LONG AS
THE BIRDS SING
I CAN

A VICIOUS CIRCLE

TO FILL THE EMPTY VOID
INSIDE OF US
AND WE FILL IT UP
WITH OTHER THINGS
TO MAKE IT FULL
AND IT NEVER STAYS FULL
IT'S ALWAYS EMPTY

A CUT

I WAS WIPING AWAY
MY TEARS ONE NIGHT
FROM A SAD DREAM
WHILE I CLEANSED
THE TEARS WITH
MY HAND I CUT
THE SKIN DEEPLY
NEAR THE WRIST
BY SOMETHING
ON MY FACE
I LOOKED SHOCKED
PUZZLED AT IT
AND SAW THAT I
SLICED OPEN MY SKIN
CAUSE OF A FROZEN TEAR
WHICH HAD HARDENED
BY SPITE

THE TUNNEL

I WAS RIDING THRU
A DARK TUNNEL
OF MY LIFE
SOME OF MY LIFE
PLEASURES I COULD
NOT RECALL
SOME OF MY LIFE
TORTURES THAT I
DID NOT WISH
TO REMEMBER
COULD NOT STOP
AND STILL I RODE
THROUGH THE
DARK TUNNEL
OF MY LIFE.
WAS THAT ME
REFLECTED IN
THE WINDOW
LOOKING BACK?
I COULD NOT TELL…

SECRETS

I KEPT
EVERYTHING
HIDDEN
FROM
EVERYONE
EVEN MYSELF
I DIDN'T KNOW
ANY BETTER
OR DID I?

REVERBERATION OF GEIST
SUN HAS FALLEN INTO A VACUUM
FINGERS OF BARREN TREES DISAPPEAR
SLOWLY A WIND BREATHES
SOON A STILL NIGHT WILL BE UPON ME
NO SOUND IN THE OXYGEN AIR
ONLY MY SOUL AND A
REVERBERATION OF GEIST
I AM ALONE

THE ORANGE MOON GLOW
FLOATING DEEP ABOVE
THE INKY VOID OF NIGHT LIQUID
HALO OF CLOUD AS IF
GHOSTS LICKING THE AIR
LIKE SONATA OF LULLABY
THE INSECT SILENTLY CRIES

CAMELS MARCHED
ACROSS THE SALT PLAINS
THE SPOTTED SKY CAME INTO VIEW
WHITE BLAZE SHIMMER HAZE
I NESTLED WATCHING
IN THE BLEAK DISTANCE
MIND DULL FLAT LINE
FROZEN METAL
FUSED INTO MY FLESH
AND THOUGH I WAS
AWARE OF THE CAMELS
THEY WERE AWARE OF
SOMETHING I WAS NOT
THEY WALKED AND WALKED FREE
TASTE OF METAL IN MY MOUTH
SOOTHE LIKE BABIES BREATH
IT'S LOVE TO MY EYES

ASIAN DREAM
ASIAN LEAVES CUT THEMSELVES
UPON THE THORNS OF THEIR
LOST SEEDLESS LOVE
THE BIRD OF LOTUS BLOSSOM
EXPLODES IN TUNE
RADIANCE OF ESSENCE
A MUFFLED CRY
OF AN ANCIENT TREE
KNOWS NOT FOR WHAT
IT CRIES FOR
THE STARS IN OSMOSIS
ARE KILLING THEIR LIGHT VIVIDLY
OR ARE MY EYES CONSCIOUSLY
GROWING DIM
THE PRAYING MANTIS CRAWLS
INTO THE WIND

SNOW IS FALLING
ON BROKEN EXPOSED NERVES
THE SILENCE IS ACHING
IN TIME LAPSE FREEZE FRAME
TREES HAVE MOVED CLOSER
AS IF WANTING COMFORT
AND THE SNOW
I CANNOT FEEL

SWIMMING IN THE
WOMB OF WORLD
I AM BLIND
CANNOT FIND AN EXIT
THE FLUID STINGS MY EYES
BUT I DO NOT WANT TO LEAVE

THE PAIN WE INFLICT
UPON OURSELVES
IS THE PAIN WE LEAST
EXPECT TO BELIEVE

SQUEEZE THE NAKED FEVER
WITH THESE SEIZURE HANDS
IN THE FUTURE A BABY CRIES
IN THE DISTANCE
IT NEEDS TO FEED
IT KNOWS NO AFFECTION BECAUSE
IT HAS NOT RECEIVED ANY YET
THE WALLS ARE RED
THE SKY FULL OF STARS
ANOTHER CRY SHATTERED THE NIGHT
IT KNOWS NO ATTENTION BECAUSE
IT HAS NOT RECEIVED ANY YET
SPECTRE GAZED AND FLOATED BY
STRANGE MEN APPEARED IN THE SKY
STARING UPON THE CHILD
AN EXPERIMENT IN THE COLD ROOM
IT KNOWS NO LOVE CAUSE
IT HAS NOT RECEIVED ANY YET
IT NEEDS TO FEED
IN THE DISTANCE
STILL IN THE FUTURE A BABY CRIES
IT KNOWS NOTHING ELSE

I USED TO SLEEP
WITH YOUR LOVE
NOW YOUR LOVE
DISINTEGRATED
IN THE PAST
THE ONLY ONE
I LAY WITH NOW
IS MY SHADOW
AND MY PAST

THIS CLOUD
THIS EVENING
REMINDS ME
OF YOUR HEART
I CANNOT GRASP IT
TO HOLD FOR MYSELF
AND I CANNOT STOP
IT FROM PASSING
STILL IT FLOATS ON BY
TO WHERE
I'LL NEVER KNOW

I REMEMBER
WHEN I MET YOU
I LOST MY FEAR
NOW YOU ARE
GONE FROM ME
AND ALL I HAVE NOW
IS MY FEAR

MY HEART
SHATTERED
IS IN FRAGMENTS
BECAUSE OF YOU
I KEEP TRYING TO
REASSEMBLE THEM
EVEN THOUGH I HAVE
NO MEMORY OF
WHERE THEY BELONG
I TRY NOT TO LOSE
A SINGLE ONE

STARS ARE ECHOING
THE BLACK BLEEDS
INTO ITSELF
A NEW YEAR
BEGINS

GHOST OF A HEART
AT EDGE OF A SEA CRIED
I WANT ANOTHER LIFE

THE CATERPILLAR
CRAWLS AS DO I
BUT THE CATERPILLAR
HAS A PURPOSE

A QUARANTINED HEART
REJECTED LOST SOUL
I BECOME WEAKER
DIAMOND CRESCENT RISING
REFLECTING A RAZORS EDGE
THIS THORN REMAINS
FOREVER

TWILIGHT OZONE
THE VIRUS OF YOUR LOVE
THE SOUL OF SEA
RESURRECTED A CRY
OF WHAT ONCE WAS
SEPARATION
ALWAYS IN MY HEART

THE SHAKING
FETUS CRIED OUT
"HOLD ME, I AM VULNERABLE."
BUT THERE WAS NO ONE TO
HOLD THE SHAKING
VULNERABLE FETUS
AND NO ONE
HEARD THE CRYING
SOAKED IN FEAR
EXCEPT FOR THE FETUS

IN THE UNKNOWN
RELAXING IN
NUMB COMFORT
I DO NOT FEEL
THE THORNS
WELL NOT ALL
THE TIME

OPAL BEAMS
OF ZENITH RIPPLE
UPON WAVES
OF THE SEA
YET A CLOUD
HAS ECLIPSED
THE ONLY STAR

MEMORIES
SILENCED
IN A SEA
OF SORROW
BUTTERFLY
WILL YOU
SING AWAKE
THE MOON

FORGETTING DESIRE
IS NOT AN EASY THING
CAN THE OCEAN
FORGET THE
REFLECTION
OF THE MOON

I SHALL NEVER KNOW
WHAT LOVE COULD HAVE BEEN
FROM THIS SINGLE TEAR

I TRIED TO IMPLANT
FEELING AND MEMORY
INTO THIS HEART
BUT I SUFFER FROM
DEFECTIVE EMOTIONS
I WISH MY MEMORY
WAS AS DEFECTIVE

OH PHANTOM
YOU'VE SOILED YOURSELF
THERE IS NO ONE AROUND
TO CLEANSE YOU
WILL THESE TEARS
TAKE AWAY THE STAIN?

FROM MY BREATH BIRD SOAR
THE STAR LIGHT OF HEAVEN
YOUR EYES DANCE IN AN
ANGELS PIROUETTE OF BILSS
MY SOUL GLIDING
UPON OCEAN OF GALAXY
SONIC HISS OF A BEATING HEART
FED FROM THE FIRES OF DESIRE
DRIFT TO SLEEP A DREAM OF LOVE
BIRTHED OUT FROM
SONATA OF HEAVEN

THE PHANTOM IS GONE
BUTTERFLY YOU CAN
COME OUT NOW AND FLY
AS YOU DID BEFORE
AND DANCE WITH THE
MORNING STAR WITHIN
A BEAUTIFUL STILLNESS

SO TORMENTING
ARE THESE GHOSTS
SO INTENSE
IS THE FEAR
AND RELUCTANCE
TO RID MYSELF OF THIS
FRACTURED PAST LOVE
SO COMFORTING
IS THE TORMENT
OF THESE GHOSTS

THIS VESSEL
IS FORGOTTEN
THIS HEART MOANS
I FEEL A VACUUM
MY SENSES SEVER
A FLOATING DISGUISE
MY SENSES REMAIN

I RECALL
THE TASTE OF
YOUR LOVE
THIS EVENING
ALTHOUGH ALONE
SALIVA FORMS
AT THIS THOUGHT
I STILL REMAIN
FAMISHED
SO STRANGE
ITS AFTERTASTE

MUSIC BY
ANGELO SPIZZARRI

RED HAZE
FUTURESHOCK
SOMNAMBULIST
MELTDOWN

ALBUMS AVAILABLE
@ AMAZON, CdBaby
& iTUNES mP3 & CD

www.SPIZZARRI.com

FOR INFORMATION
ON MUSIC, BOOKS &
OTHER EVENTS
PLEASE VISIT THESE
WEBSITES BELOW:

WWW.SPIZZARRI.COM
FACEBOOK.COM/SPIZZARRI
INSTAGRAM.COM/SPIZZARRI
TWITTER.COM/SPIZZARRI

"REALITY IS ONES OWN PERCEPTION."

www.SPIZZARRI.com

www.ingramcontent.com/pod-product-compliance
Lightning Source LLC
Chambersburg PA
CBHW020658300426
44112CB00007B/430